Thinking skills

Geography and Sustainable Development

Patricia Kendell

A1070765

HOPSCOTCH
EDUCATIONAL PUBLISHING

WWF-UK registered charity number 1081247
A company limited by guarantee number 4016725
Panda symbol © 1986 WWF
® WWF registered trademark owner

Published by Hopscotch
A division of MA Education Ltd
St Jude's Church, Dulwich Road
Herne Hill, London SE24 0PB
Tel: 020 7738 5454

© 2008 Hopscotch Educational Publishing

Written by Patricia Kendell
Series design by Blade Communications
Illustrated by Sarah Wimperis and Brian Lee
Cover illustrated by Pat Murray
Printed in the UK by CLE-print

This book was printed on recycled paper.

Patricia Kendell hereby asserts her moral right to be identified as
the author of this work in accordance with the Copyright, Designs
and Patents Act, 1988.

ISBN 978-1-904307-49-5

Key Stage One

Key Stage Two

Thinking skills and geography

Aim of this book

The aim of this publication is to make more explicit the place of thinking skills in the teaching and learning of geography and sustainable development for children aged 5 to 11 years, and to demonstrate how this relates to the achievement of the aims of the school curricula in all the countries of the UK.

Thinking skills underpin good primary practice in all subject areas. Promoting these skills helps to empower young children to become independent learners and to prepare them for taking up their role as well informed, constructively critical citizens. They are essential to education for sustainable development (ESD), which in the last few years has been integrated into the curricula of all UK countries in varying ways, as awareness of our global links and responsibilities has permeated our collective consciousness.

'...[the school curriculum] should develop their awareness and understanding of, and respect for, the environments in which they live, and secure their commitment to sustainable development at a personal, local and global level.'
The National Curriculum: Handbook for primary teachers in England, 2000

Thinking skills

Information processing skills

- Locating and collecting relevant information
- Sorting
- Classifying
- Sequencing
- Comparing and contrasting
- Analysing relationships

Reasoning skills

- Giving reasons for opinions and actions
- Drawing inferences
- Making deductions
- Explaining what they think
- Making judgements, informed by reasons and evidence

Enquiry skills

- Asking relevant questions
- Posing and defining problems
- Planning what to do
- How to research
- Predicting outcomes
- Anticipating consequences
- Testing conclusions
- Improving ideas

Creative thinking skills

- Generating and extending ideas
- Suggesting hypotheses
- Applying imagination
- Looking for innovative outcomes

Evaluation skills

- Evaluating information
- Judging the value of what the learner reads, hears and does
- Developing criteria for judging the value of their own and others' work or ideas

The study of geography enables children to develop a range of thinking skills, particularly those needed to develop an understanding of sustainable development. Children can be encouraged to use their thinking skills to:

- study places from local to global to explore the interdependence of society, economy and the natural environment;
- study how people are influenced by, and affect environments;
- develop a sense of responsibility for personal and group action;
- develop an appreciation of the need for sustainable use and management of resources for present and future generations;
- be able to listen carefully to arguments from different viewpoints.

Reference: *Lessons in Life: Resources for primary school teachers*
Published by Shell Education Service for project partners (CEE, Field Studies Council, SEEC; WWF-UK)

'In 1987 the United Nations Brundtland report to the World Commission on Environment and Development defined sustainable development as:

"Development which meets the needs of the present without compromising the ability of future generations to meet their own needs".'

Key concepts of Education for Sustainable Development

Interdependence
Understanding how people, the environment and the economy are inextricably linked at all levels from local to global.

Citizenship and stewardship
Recognising the importance of taking individual responsibility to ensure the world is a better place.

Needs and rights of future generations
Understanding our own basic needs and the implications of actions taken today on the needs of future generations.

Diversity
Respecting and valuing both human diversity – cultural, social, economic – and biodiversity.

Quality of life
Acknowledging that global equity and justice are essential elements of sustainability and that basic needs must be met universally.

Sustainable change
Understanding that resources are finite and that this has implications for people's lifestyles, and for commerce and industry.

Care and caution
Acknowledging that there is a range of possible approaches to sustainability and that situations are constantly changing, indicating a need for flexibility and lifelong learning.

Reference: A Report to DfEE/QCA from the panel for Education for Sustainable Development, 14 September 1998
Down to Earth: A Scottish perspective on sustainable development.
February 1999

Activity ideas

The following chapters are based on units from the schemes of work to support the English National Curriculum for geography, but the themes are generic and the examples of activities to engage children in the development of thinking skills can be adapted to meet the particular needs of pupils and teachers throughout the UK. Most of these activities will be familiar to teachers and will already form part of more extended schemes of work. However, the purpose here is to highlight relevant thinking skills in the process of extending children's knowledge and understanding.

Tips and suggestions

You might find it useful to refer to these as you work through the activity ideas.

Thinking skill strategies

Brainstorming

Brainstorming is a technique that helps to release and record creative thoughts. Here are some tips for successful brainstorming.

- Keep the objective simple and clearly focused.
- Make sure the children are clear about the subject/purpose of the session.
- Keep it short; five to ten minutes is long enough.
- Record everything.
- Do not make judgements about ideas – they are all useful.
- Encourage lateral thinking and unusual ideas.
- Small group sizes of about five are ideal, but brainstorming with a whole class can work well; for example, at the start of a project to find out what the children already know, what they want to find out and how they might set about this.

Brainstorming is a particularly useful technique for getting children to formulate questions. Use the examples of questions in the Enquiry and Fieldwork section on the facing page to provide the children with a framework for formulating their own questions.

Circle time

Circle time is simply a way of structuring class discussion time. It can be used for many purposes, including helping children develop their thinking skills and express their ideas and feelings in a non-threatening environment. Here are a few ground rules:

- Everyone's position is equal.
- It is a time for children's own concerns.
- Everyone has a responsibility to listen and an opportunity to speak.
- Exclusion from circle time is not used as a sanction for previous bad behaviour, since this affects the children who need this experience the most.
- Children have a right to 'pass'. There is no pressure to speak but those who do are listened to without ridicule.
- Children who choose not to speak should be no less valued than those who do. Circle time may deal with challenging issues but it is not a test.
- Circle time becomes motivating because it is child-centred and personally relevant. Taking part is its own reward and praise for speaking introduces a pressure to perform.

Circle time can help children develop responsible rather than conformist behaviour. It provides a model for a more equal society.

Source: www.circletime.co.uk

Plenary sessions

If children have been working in groups it is helpful to bring them together to discuss what they have been doing. The natural time for this is when the children have completed a specific task, but it can also be a useful technique for refocusing an activity. A plenary session enables children to:

- summarise what they have learned;
- share this learning;
- check that they have been on task, ie that they understood the original task or brief;
- raise questions about what they have learned;
- agree what they need to do, or find out, next.

Specific geography skills and tools

Graphicacy

Graphicacy is a key geography skill focused on the use of maps. Photographs and aerial photographs, compasses, the Internet and ICT packages can also be used.

Graphicacy tasks, progressively, may include:

- children placing toys in the correct positions on a play mat; for example, car in garage or fire engine in fire station;
- making a track map of, say, a model railway, then drawing it;
- using a local map to plot the route to school and adding features observed;
- alpha-numerical referencing of home, school and other known features on a map;
- sequencing photographs on a map, for example those of a river from source to mouth;
- plotting directions and distances, for example schools in the netball league;
- using four figure and six figure Ordnance Survey grid references for other schools;
- orientating maps to north in the school grounds, and making signpost map of features;
- using maps and compasses in orienteering exercises in and beyond the school grounds;
- map reading and annotating simple fieldwork sketches, using symbols, key, scale and so on.

Source: Chapter 7 (Peter Bloomfield and Bernice Rawlings)
Excellence in Education 2001 – The Primary School Curriculum
ed Brundrett M et al. Publisher: Peter Francis

Enquiry and Fieldwork

These are essential learning tools in geography. Fieldwork seeks to explain and make sense of the real world and help children see the wonder and beauty of the world around them.

The fundamentals of geographical enquiry include:

- providing resources such as maps, aerial photographs, newspaper articles and audio-visual materials;
- providing fieldwork opportunities with appropriate enquiry tasks;

- setting tasks that stimulate investigation by using key words and questions to promote investigation, such as:
  - Why do people park in these roads?
  - How is the coast used in this area?
  - When is the park used; is it all day, every day of the year?
  - What do the map and the photographs tell us about how the land was used?
- higher order thinking, which can be promoted by such questions as:
  - What if the school wanted to build some new classrooms over the pond and the corner of the football pitch?
  - When would you think it was all right to cut down the forests?

Source: ibid

The local area

Around our school

Objective

- To use thinking skills to explore what children like and dislike about their local environment.

Resources

- Photographs and pictures of the local area
- A good clear local map (for example, from your local authority or an estate agent). Enough copies for each child and an enlargement for display purposes
- Digital camera(s) for the children
- Clipboards and drawing equipment
- Research on the route to be taken by the children

Introduction

Most young children begin to develop their geographical skills, knowledge and understanding by exploring local environments. This activity idea highlights how thinking skills are implicit in this familiar early introduction to geography.

Tell the children that they are going to find out and discuss what their local area looks like.

Information processing skills

❑ Give groups of children a number of pictures of your local area to work with. Do they know where these pictures were taken? Organise a walk around the area to see how many of the places illustrated they can locate.

❑ Help the children to take their own photographs of places and buildings along the route, such as a church, postbox, interesting gateway and overflowing litter bin!

❑ Back in class, trace the journey on the enlarged map and make a display to show where all the pictures, including those taken by the children, fit on the map.

Enquiry skills

❑ Brainstorm questions the children would like to ask about the pictures. For example:
- Is this church (old parish church) older than the church near the shops (new church)?
- Who collects the litter?
- What building might have been behind the old gateway? Are there any clues?

(For more information and ideas on brainstorming see pages 6 and 7.)

❑ Add these to the display.

❑ Talk about how the children might find answers to their questions. Whom could they ask? Perhaps a local resident, shopkeeper, neighbour or relative who has lived there a long time. Where could they look for information? The local library or museum, the town hall or guidebooks on the locality. Invite someone to the classroom to talk to the children and answer their questions.

Reasoning skills

❑ Ask the children to sort the pictures under different headings, such as:
  - what happens there (home, shop, public building/space)
  - which pictures they like/dislike ('I like the pattern the bricks in the wall make,' and 'I don't like the shopping centre because it is noisy and people drop litter.' Sensitivity is needed if the area covered includes any child's home.)

❑ Can the children explain why they have sorted the pictures in the way they have?

Evaluation skills

❑ Hold a circle time plenary session with the whole class in order to review children's likes and dislikes about their local area, and how these feelings might have changed in the course of their work. Give each child an opportunity to talk about a picture. How does it make them feel? Happy, excited, sad, annoyed, angry, puzzled and so on? Do any of the other children agree? Invite other opinions and let the children discuss them.

Links with the Geography Scheme of Work

This activity has direct links with Unit 1, 'Around our school – the local area'. In particular it addresses the learning objectives 'What can we see in the streets around our school?' and 'What are our immediate surroundings like?'

ESD focus

This activity helps children to begin to develop their role as citizens. They are encouraged to express their likes and dislikes about their immediate environment in preparation for developing informed opinions about looking after and improving it.

Thinking skills: Geography and ESD

The local area

A trip to the park

Objective

- To use a range of thinking skills to investigate the features of a park.

Resources

- Photocopiable Sheet 1 (page 46)
- Photos of your local park

Introduction

A study of the school environment could be extended to a study of a specific local environment, such as a named street or the local park. Taking the children to a local park is the ideal, but if this is impractical use the illustration of the park provided on page 46, or take some photos of your local park to use as a focus for the development of thinking skills. The following activity ideas are based on the illustration, but they can be adapted for a visit to a real park.

Enquiry skills

❑ Before you show the children the illustration or photos of a park, use questions such as the following to elicit what they already know:
  – What do you know about parks?
  – Who goes to a park?
  – What would you like to find out about your local park?
  – What facilities might be there? (Café, toilets.)
  – What might be available for children to use?
  – Are there any sporting activities undertaken in the park?

Information processing skills

❑ Organise the children into small groups and give each group a copy of the illustration of a park or the photos of your park. Ask them to write down what they can see; for example that there are trees, flowers, animals, birds, people, buildings, play equipment, pond and paths. What are the people in the park doing? (Playing games, sitting, walking, and so on.)

❑ Ask the groups to discuss the differences and the similarities between the illustration and a park in their local area. If you are using photos of the local park show them the illustration at this stage and ask what similarities and differences they can see. What can they see in the illustration that is not in their park? What is in their park, but not in the illustration? What is in both?

❑ Ask the children to make a plan of one of the parks (the illustrated one or the one they know), indicating all the main features, such as paths, pond, play area and benches.

Reasoning and information processing skills

❑ Extend the children's observations by asking them questions such as:

- Do you think this park is suitable for your family?
- Do you think this park is suitable for everyone's family?
- What features should be there for different groups of people – young children, teenagers or old people? Why?
- How could you find out about what the park offers for these different groups?
- How would you record the information?

Reasoning and creative thinking skills

❑ Ask the children to have another close look at the illustration. Hold a plenary session to elicit what they have found out about the main features of this park. What do these features tell them about who uses the park, how it is used and when? Can they suggest reasons for the similarities and the differences between this park and their local park?

❑ Ask them to draw a picture to show how they would improve this park.

Thinking skills: Geography and ESD

The local area

How can we make it safer?

Objective

- To use thinking skills to identify what makes the local area dangerous and what can be done to make it safer.

Resources

- Clipboards
- Photocopiable Sheets 2 and 3 (pages 47 and 48)
- A good clear local map

Introduction

Investigating local traffic is often used to develop geographical skills in a familiar environment. It can also help develop a range of thinking skills.

Tell the children that today they are going to consider the traffic in and around their local area.

Enquiry skills

❏ What do the children think about the traffic near the school? Hold a brainstorming session and record their ideas. Useful questions include:
  - Is it busy and noisy, or quiet?
  - Does the air smell nice or nasty?
  - Is it safe to cross the road?
  - Are there problems with parking?
  - Are the problems mentioned worse at different times of the day?

❏ Ask the children how they think they could find out more about any problems they have raised.

Information processing skills

❏ Take the children outside and ask them to look for all the things they can see to control traffic and parking. Give them copies of photocopiable Sheet 2 (page 47) to help them collect the information. Back in class make a large map of the street surveyed and ask the children to place their symbols (or draw their own) for the traffic/parking mechanisms where they saw them.

❏ If possible let the children go outside and survey the traffic at different times of the day. They will need to be supervised, so you could use the services of a parent or classroom assistant for this. Let them do this for periods of around 20 minutes. Before they go, discuss with them what they are going to look out for and how they might record what they see. Show them how to tally. Give them copies of photocopiable Sheet 3 (page 48) on which to record what they see.

Reasoning skills

❏ Together, look at the picture map the children have made. What do they think about the methods that are currently used around their school to control and calm traffic and to control parking? Do they work? Ask them to explain their reasoning.

Creative thinking skills

❏ Brainstorm innovative ideas for helping to solve any problems. The children could add their solutions to the street map.

Links with the Geography Scheme of Work

This activity is closely related to the learning objectives in Unit 2, 'How can we make the area around our school safer?'

ESD focus

This activity helps children develop a concern and care for issues that affect everyone who travels past their school. It is a first step towards developing the knowledge and skills to address the issue of how sustainable current transport policy is, and what changes might be needed to meet the needs of future generations.

Other places in the UK

Objectives

• To find out how and why the seaside is different from another place.

Resources

• Photocopiable Sheet 4 (page 49)
• Photographs of a specific seaside place
• Maps and atlases
• Flip-chart to record responses

The seaside

Introduction

Children's understanding of place can be broadened by a study of a different place to that where they live. The seaside is a popular topic. If you can't take the children on a visit, then try this activity idea using the illustration. Those of you who live by the seaside could do the same activities but for a place inland, perhaps a city.

Enquiry and information processing skills

❑ Give the children copies of the illustration of the seaside on photocopiable Sheet 4 (page 49). Ask them the following questions:
  – Does anyone know where this place is?
  – Has anyone been to a place like this?

❑ The last question could be developed by asking, 'Where is the nearest seaside?'

❑ Use a map and help the children find a seaside place. Ask 'Has anyone been there?' Let those children who have describe what they saw there. Write their descriptions on a large piece of paper.

❑ Ask the children how they might get to this place. Refer to the map again to identify rail and road routes.

Reasoning skills

❏ Refer back to the illustration and, using the information gathered in the enquiry session, ask the children why a seaside place is like this. Answers might include: 'People need somewhere to stay, eat, fish, swim, go on holiday, have fun and so on.' Encourage them to think about how people have changed this place to meet their needs.

❏ How is the seaside the same as, and different from, the place where the children live? Ask the children why. 'It is different because…'; 'It is the same because…'

Creative thinking

❏ Ask the children to think about what it would be like to live at the seaside. They might like going to the seaside for a holiday, but would it be the same if they lived there all the time? Pose questions such as:
  – What would it be like in winter?
  – What would it be like going to school near the seaside? Would it be any different from where you go to school now?
  – What would it be like if you lived there and enjoyed all the different places and then in the summer your special places were invaded by visitors?

❏ Finally, ask the children to imagine this scenario: What would happen if everybody decided to move to the seaside because they liked the fresh air? They should think about the following:
  – What would happen in the towns and cities inland?
  – What would happen at the coasts?
  – Where would people live?
  – Would there be enough houses?
  – Would there be enough schools?
  – Are there any industries we need inland that would disappear?
  – What would happen to wild places and wildlife at the coast?

Links with the Geography Scheme of Work

This activity has direct links with the first three learning objectives in Unit 4, 'Going to the seaside'.

ESD focus

This activity provides a starting point for children to think about how people affect the environment either where they live or as tourists. It also provides opportunities to develop a respect for the diversity of human needs.

The wider world

Going on holiday

Objectives

- To use enquiry skills to find places on the atlas visited by friends.

- To record how these places are reached.

- To discuss what makes a good holiday.

Resources

- Holiday brochures
- Holiday photographs
- Large world map
- Atlas or globe
- Photocopiable Sheet 5 (page 50)

Introduction

Talking about holidays and where people go widens still further children's awareness of other places and how they are similar and different.

Enquiry skills

❑ Ask the children where they have been on holiday (this needs sensitive handling as some children might not have holidays, but days out can be used too). Encourage them to think about whether the place is in this country or another country. Is it a hot or a cold place? Is it by the seaside or near a river in the country? Is it a big city, a small town or a village? It might be a local park, zoo or theme park. Find these places in an atlas or on a globe. Mark them on the large world map.

❑ Ask the children to list some of the things to see and do at these holiday places. These might include sand to make sandcastles, rock pools, seagulls, swimming, visits to interesting places, such as a castle. (Answers can be based on knowledge as well as speculation – it might be best to have two headings.)

❑ Talk about how we get to these places. Discuss the different transport methods and add them to the map, using sticky notes with either words or symbols on them.

❑ Talk about in the wayw in which each place is different and why this might be so.

Reasoning, negotiation and evaluation skills

❏ Give each child the writing/drawing frame on Sheet 5 (page 50). Tell them they have to think about where they would **like** to go on holiday and then write about it and draw pictures of it on the frame. This could be a place they have been to, somewhere they have heard of or even an imaginary place.

❏ Organise the children into small groups to share these worksheets. Tell each group that they have to discuss the different ideas, then agree on one of them as the place for the holiday this year.

I think we should go to Greece because it will be hot.

❏ Give them a little time to talk about this and then ask one child from each group to say where they have decided to go. Ask the groups to explain to the class how and why they came to their decision.

Links with the Geography Scheme of Work

This activity relates to the last learning objective in Unit 4, 'Going to the seaside', and touches upon many of the learning objectives in Unit 5, 'Where in the world is Barnaby Bear?'

ESD focus

This activity helps develop children's thinking about what we mean by quality of life and how this can mean different things for different people. It also provides children with an opportunity to negotiate with others reaching a decision that takes account of the diversity of need in the group.

Finding out about another place

Objectives

- To use enquiry skills to find out about a different country.

- To ask questions about how and why life for people there is different from life in this country.

Resources

- Photocopiable Sheets 6 to 8 (pages 51 to 53)

- Large world map

- A map of Ghana

- Books and photos of Ghanaian life in cities and villages such as Accra

Introduction

This activity idea is based on a case study from Oxfam. By reading about Anusibuno, a seven-year-old Ghanaian girl, children can begin to appreciate the similarities and differences between her life and their own. The ideas are generic and could be used with other case studies and photopacks currently available.

Information processing skills

❏ Read the story of Anusibuno to the whole class. Ask them if they know where Ghana is. Find it on a large wall map. Talk about what the children think Ghana might be like. Make a list of these ideas on a flip-chart. Then give the children access to photos and books about Ghana to check if their ideas were correct.

❏ Organise the children into groups and give each group a copy of the case study (pages 51 and 52). Ask them to discuss in what ways Anusibuno's life is the same as theirs. Make a list of the similarities, such as living in a house with her family, going to school and playing with her friends.

❏ Then ask the children to think about how Anusibuno's life is different from theirs. Ask each group to use words and pictures to note down these differences on photocopiable Sheet 8 (page 53).

Reasoning skills

❏ Ask the groups to think about the following question: 'Do you think that Anusibuno's life would be more like yours if she lived in a big town like Accra?' Identify where Accra is on the map and show the children pictures taken of life in Accra. Ask them to come up with some reasons, such as: 'I think Anusibuno's life would be more like ours if she lived in Accra because there would be shops and buses.'

❏ In what ways might it still be different? Answers might include: 'It would still be different because it is very hot in Ghana and there are different fruits and vegetables to eat.'

Evaluation skills

❏ Pin up the worksheets from each group. Hold a plenary session to discuss the differences and the similarities between their lives and Anusibuno's life. Have any of the groups come up with similar points? If there are differences, ask the children to discuss these and say whether they agree or disagree with them.

❏ Do the same with the answers to the question 'Do you think that Anusibuno's life would be more like yours if she lived in a big town like Accra?' Discuss points of agreement and disagreement. Is life in big cities much the same all over the world? Is the difference between living in a village and living in a town greater in Ghana than in the UK?

Links with the Geography Scheme of Work

This activity is loosely related to learning objectives in Unit 3, 'An island home', using the case study of Anusibuno instead of the story of Katie Morag. It also covers some of the learning objectives in Unit 4, 'Where in the World is Barnaby Bear?'.

ESD focus

This activity provides an insight into the life of a child in another part of the world with all the opportunities to appreciate how and why her life is different from, and similar to, that of a UK child. It is a step towards developing respect for and valuing human diversity, and knowing how human impact on the environment differs around the world.

Investigating the local area

How is our locality changing?

Introduction

Work done at Key Stage 1 to explore the local environment can be extended during Key Stage 2 to include the change over time dimension.

Enquiry skills

❏ Brainstorm questions children could ask about their locality, such as:
  – How has the locality changed over time?
  – How can we find out?
  – Is it still changing now?
  – What has disappeared from the area?
  – How would we like our locality to change in the future?
  – What can we do to make the local area a better place in which to live?

Information processing skills

❏ Give the children time and facilities for research, perhaps using the local library, school archives and a local website. They could draw up a questionnaire for long-term residents of the local area.

❏ Encourage the children to plan how best to record the changes they have discovered. They will need to agree the key features they wish to track. They could use the recording sheet on page 54.

❏ Using the information they have found, ask the children to suggest possible reasons why these changes have occurred. For example, the houses that the long-term residents remember in a particular street may have been knocked down to make way for a supermarket, an office block or a carpark.

Objectives

• To use a range of thinking skills to discover how the local area has changed over time.

• To critically evaluate ideas for future development.

Resources

• Access to local history resources

• Photocopiable Sheet 9 (page 54)

Reasoning and creative thinking skills

❏ Organise the children into groups and ask each group to discuss what they think their locality might look like in 100 years' time. They can make a map of how it might look with drawings and explanatory text.

❏ Use questions such as these to help them generate and extend their ideas:
- Do you think people will like living here then?
- What will be good about it?
- What might not be so good?
- Who will benefit and who will lose as a result of the changes?
- Would you like to live here then?

Evaluation skills

❏ Let each group present its map to the class, talking through how and why they came to these conclusions about the future, and answering questions put to them by the others.

❏ It might be possible to display these pictorial maps somewhere in school, with a box for comments and ideas from other children.

Links with the Geography Scheme of Work

This activity supports the last learning objective in Unit 6, 'Investigating the local area: What changes have taken place in the village?'

ESD focus

This activity enables children to explore changes in their environment and to consider how the actions they take now or the decisions they make might affect the quality of life for future generations.

Investigating the local area

Objectives

- To use enquiry and reasoning skills to explore land use.

- To think creatively about alternative plans, critically evaluating their merits.

Resources

- Photocopiable Sheets 10 and 11 (pages 55 and 56)

Land use

Introduction

Another aspect of exploring the local environment is investigating land use. You might create a scenario based on a real local issue where there is a conflict of interests regarding the development of a piece of land. Alternatively you could use the scenario described in this activity.

Enquiry skills

❑ Discuss a local issue where there is a conflict of interests over the use of a piece of land. Or read the scenario on Sheet 10 (page 55) to the children.

❑ Discuss the scenario with the children. Brainstorm the possible different interest groups:
  - the council;
  - local shopkeepers;
  - superstore management;
  - old people;
  - families;
  - market stall owners.

Reasoning and creative thinking skills

❑ Brainstorm questions to tease out the issues, such as:

 – Will the new shopping centre mean more cars in the town?

 – What impact will this have on people and the environment?

 – Do people need more shops? What type of shops?

 – Are there more pressing needs in the community? (For example, more leisure/arts facilities or green spaces.)

 – Could the market be developed to attract more custom? (Maybe it could become a farmers' market to sell local and organic produce.)

❑ Allocate the role cards (photocopiable Sheet 11 on page 56). Give the children time to get into role – allow some research time if necessary and then hold the meeting.

Reasoning and evaluation skills

❑ Hold a plenary session to debrief, using questions such as:

 – What was the outcome of the discussion?

 – Was there agreement on the way forward?

 – Who will gain from the decision? Who will lose?

 – Who had the most powerful arguments? Why?

 – How did each group feel during the discussion?

Links with the Geography Scheme of Work

Land use issues can be found in several units, but this activity relates most closely to the last learning objective in Unit 8, 'Improving the environment: What is this place like and why? How can it be improved?'

ESD focus

This role-play activity is about understanding that decisions taken now can have profound social, economic and cultural effects. It also helps children understand that people have different views on sustainability issues and that these may often lead to conflict. Therefore they need to be able to listen to arguments and weigh evidence carefully.

Waste and recycling

Objectives

- To investigate what happens to waste material in school and in the local community.

- To present creative, well reasoned suggestions for how things could be improved.

Resources

- Access to the Internet

- Books about waste and recycling

- Photocopiable Sheet 12 (page 57)

Introduction

Investigating what produces waste and how we deal with it is a popular project for schools as part of a unit of work on improving the environment. The following activity can be used to focus on thinking skills.

Information processing and reasoning skills

❑ Give the children copies of the photocopiable sheet on page 57 to do by way of introducing the topic of recycling. Tell them to sort items illustrated into those made from aluminium, plastic, glass and paper, and then to answer the questions.

❑ Discuss the children's answers. The correct answers are: paper – trees; glass – sand (plus other minerals); aluminium – the mineral bauxite; plastic – petroleum (mostly). Make the point that all these products come out of the earth. Making them involves using different types of energy and many human skills.

❑ To stimulate thought about how and when we use resources, ask the children to look round the classroom. Use the following questions to get them thinking:
  – What things in our classroom are necessary for us to be here and learn?
  – How long do they last?
  – Who supplies them?
  – Where do they come from?
  – Who pays?
  – Can we make them last longer?
  – Is it worth it?
  – What effects does manufacturing these resources have on the environment?
  – Are some of the resources more vital than others?
  – Do we really need everything here?
  – Do we waste things?
  – What could we do without?

❑ Divide the class into groups and ask each group to investigate one resource each – paper, wood, plastic, aluminium or glass. Give the groups time to do some research on their resources using books and websites.

❑ They could carry out an audit of the use of one resource in the class (or school). Devise a questionnaire, such as the one on the facing page, with the children using questions agreed by the class based on their discussion.

❑ Analyse the results of the audit with the children. Are they surprised by some of their findings?

Creative thinking skills

❏ Ask the children to continue working in their groups. They should discuss and agree ideas for how their resource can be better used. Recycling is important, but it is better to find ways of reducing consumption or reusing things. For example, can they suggest ways of using less paper? Which of these resources can be reused? Can a wooden desk or chair be repaired rather than sent to the dump? In groups, ask them to come up with some ideas for improving the use of their resource. They could use a table like the one below to help them think.

Reduce	Re-use	Repair	Recycle

❏ Encourage them to be creative – how can cans, bottles, paper and plastic packaging be reused to extend their life?

Evaluation skills

❏ In a plenary session, compare and discuss the suggestions from the groups. Encourage the children to ask questions of each other in order to evaluate the ideas. Are the suggestions practical? Will they save money and energy? Who or what will benefit most from the suggestions?

❏ The class could agree on a campaign to reduce the use of one (or more) of the resources they have researched in their school. Let them discuss what they will need – a poster maybe and some information leaflets to distribute.

Paper use questionnaire

1. Is the paper we use in school made from recycled paper?

   YES   NO

2. What happens to waste paper in our school?

3. How many photocopies do we make:
   in our class? _____
   in the school office? _____
   in the whole school? _____

4. Does everyone always use both sides of a piece of paper?

Links with the Geography Scheme of Work

This activity relates closely to the first three learning objectives in Unit 8, 'Improving the environment'.

ESD focus

This activity helps children to develop the ability to distinguish between actions and products that are wasteful and those that are more sustainable. It also helps them to take responsibility for their own actions.

Traffic issues

Introduction

This activity idea builds on work done at Key Stage 1. It is designed to help the children analyse issues arising from traffic in the local area, enabling them to use and develop a range of thinking skills.

Information processing skills

❏ Carry out a survey of traffic in the local area. You could use the recording sheet on page 48 for this. Are there any issues with the traffic here? Ask the children to take photographs and map the area to show where they think the main problems lie.

Enquiry and reasoning skills

❏ Back in class, organise the children into groups. Ask the groups to think more deeply about the reasons for the problems they have noted. For each one, use a question format like this:
   – What is the problem?
   – Where exactly is it a problem?
   – Why is it a problem?
   – Why is it important to do something about it? (They should think about the political, social, economic and environmental dimensions.)
   – What are the background factors to this problem? (Poor public transport, working parents, conflicting needs of pedestrians and motorists and so on.)
   – What groups/individuals are involved?

Objectives

- To analyse the causes of a local traffic problem.
- To think through the consequences of a range of possible solutions.

Resources

- Clipboards
- Digital cameras

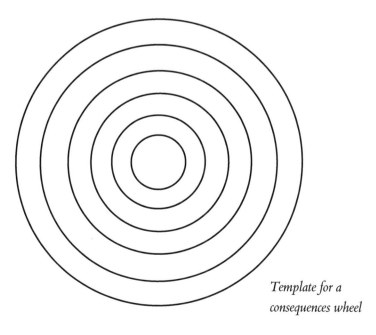

Template for a consequences wheel

Enquiry and creative thinking skills

❑ Next, the groups should brainstorm possible solutions to the issues. Useful framework questions might be:

- What alternative solutions are there?
- What are their advantages and disadvantages?
- How will the decision be made?
- Who will make it?

❑ People have many needs and services, such as play streets (a traffic-free area devoted to children), a home delivery service from supermarkets, the delivery of goods to local shops and the school run. The children should think about the impact of such needs when making their suggestions.

❑ On a blank sheet of paper, draw a 'consequences wheel' (as shown on the facing page). Make copies of it and give them to the groups. Ask each group to decide on one solution to the problems they have identified. They should write this in the centre circle. Write the immediate effects of this action around the circle. Each is linked to the central point by a line to show that they are the first consequences to arise from the action. The children should discuss what consequences may follow from the first ones. These second order consequences can be linked to those from which they flow. Succeeding third and fourth order consequences can be explored and marked in a similar fashion. Possible solutions might include:

- Banning traffic from the centre of town
- Encouraging a 'walking bus' policy for coming to school
- A bypass
- Better bus service
- Cycle tracks

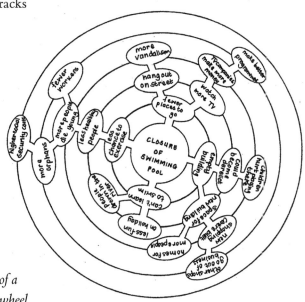

An example of a consequences wheel

Links with the Geography Scheme of Work

This activity supports the learning objectives in Unit 12, 'Should the high street be closed to traffic?' It also supports the issue based thinking in Unit 20, 'Local traffic – an environmental issue'.

ESD focus

This activity has a clear sustainability theme. It allows children to identify issues of concern to a community and think through the consequences of actions taken now on the needs and rights of future generations.

Settlements

Early settlers

Objectives

- To analyse the physical features that settlements share.

- To discuss what this tells us about human needs.

Resources

- Maps of an area with a number of villages

- Photocopiable Sheet 13 (page 58)

Introduction

This topic gives children practice in using and interpreting maps and developing analytic thinking skills.

Reasoning skills

❑ Brainstorm with the children the things they think are important to their lives – remind them of the need to eat, drink and so on. Their list might include a warm home, friendship, clean water, television, holidays and green spaces (parks, gardens, countryside). Make a list of these.

❑ Discuss what basic needs are – the things we must have in order to survive, such as food, shelter, water and fuel. Explain that these are basic needs. Highlight or underline things from the original list that are basic needs.

❑ Now ask the children to suggest which items are not essential – 'wants' as opposed to 'needs'. (Television, holidays and so on.)

Information processing skills

❑ Copy maps of a particular area of the country. This could be the county where you live. Give these to the children and ask them to look for the geographical features that might have attracted people to settle in the villages in this area. Remind them to think about the basic needs they identified.

❑ Agree that, if a basic need is to have water, then early settlers might have settled near water. Tell the children they are going to investigate different settlements on a map and why they might be where they are.

❑ Organise the children into groups and give each group a copy of photocopiable Sheet 13 (page 58). Read the list of geographical features with them and talk about what the advantages of each might have been for early settlers. For example, being near the coast could be useful for travel along the coast or overseas and being near a fort or castle would mean the settlers would have somewhere to go in the event of war.

❑ Tell the children to choose the names of four places on their map and write those four names at the top of the columns on their sheets. They should then tick or make a mark of some sort opposite each geographical feature if it occurs in their chosen place. They can add to the geographical features in the left-hand column if they want to.

Creative thinking skills

❑ Ask each child to imagine they are an early settler. Ask them to write the story of how they found this place and why they thought it was a good place in which to settle.

Links with the Geography Scheme of Work

This activity supports the first two learning objectives in Unit 9, 'Village settlers', which are about finding evidence for why early settlements developed where they did.

ESD focus

This activity develops understanding of the universality of basic human needs. From this children can develop understanding that there are differences in the extent to which people's basic needs are met.

Settlements

Objectives

- To use a range of thinking skills to discover the particular features of a settlement in a different part of the world.
- To map these differences.
- To analyse how and why this place is similar to, or different from, a known settlement.

Resources

- Photocopiable Sheets 14 to 17 (pages 59 to 62)
- Highlighter pens

A village in Togo

Introduction

Building on the work at Key Stage 1 based on the Ghanaian case study, this more in-depth study of a whole village called Ténéga in Togo helps to develop understanding of the similarities and differences between settlements around the world.

Information processing skills

❑ Tell the children that they are going to find out about a village in Togo. Do they know where Togo is? Locate it on a map.

❑ Give pairs of children copies of the case study on pages 59 to 61 to read together. When they have finished, ask them for the name of the village and the names of the five neighbourhoods. Write these on the board.

❑ Organise the children into five groups and allocate to each group one of the neighbourhoods. Tell them to read the text again, highlighting the main features of their neighbourhood. Discuss and agree these as a whole class.

❑ Now give out copies of photocopiable Sheet 17 (page 62) and ask them to put in the main features of each neighbourhood.

Reasoning skills

❑ Ask the children why they think the founder, Ti'a Nadada made his home in this place. How did it fulfil his basic needs? What did the place have that could be developed to enable a community to grow and develop here?

❑ What features in the neighbourhoods of Ténéga are the same as the place where the children live? Answers should include such things as houses, churches, schools and clinics. What features in the neighbourhoods of Ténéga are not the same? Answers will probably include such things as lack of roads, traffic, shops, supermarkets and leisure centres.

❑ Use the following questions to help the children think more deeply about the sustainability of the lifestyle of people in Ténéga.

- Think about the people in the place where you live and compare them with the people of Ténéga. Do you think the people of Ténéga are happier or less happy? Why?
- Do you think that the work the people of Ténéga do to earn a living is harmful to the natural environment?
- Do you think Ténéga is a healthy place to live? (They should think about sources of pollution, disease and availability of medical care.)

- What would happen to the people of Ténéga if the rainy season was very short?
- What contact do you think the people of Ténéga have with the rest of Togo? With other parts of Africa? With the rest of the world?
- Do you think that the next generation of people in Ténéga will be happy with the present way of life?

Creative thinking skills

❑ Divide the class into two groups. One group is to imagine they are a young person in Ténéga, and the other a young person in the UK. Ask each group to write down their fears and hopes for the future.

❑ Use circle time to allow each child, still in role, to express their main hope and their main fear for the future. When everyone has had a turn, ask for comments. Are similar hopes and fears being expressed? Are there any big differences between the hopes and fears for the future in Togo and those in the UK? If so, can the children offer any explanations?

Links with the Geography Scheme of Work

This activity provides an alternative case study for Unit 10, 'A village in India'. It covers the same learning objectives, but in a different part of the world.

ESD focus

Studying a different place can help children think through what is, and what is not, sustainable about their own community and personal lifestyle. This activity also highlights the fact that we live in an increasingly interdependent world in terms of trade and technology, and that there is much greater contact between different cultures than in the past.

Water

Where does our water come from?

Objectives

- To use enquiry skills to find out where water comes from, how it is used and where it goes.

- To evaluate water use and suggest ways to save water.

Resources

- Photocopiable Sheets 18 and 19 (pages 63 and 64)

- Access to the Internet

Introduction

The water cycle is a key concept in geography. It is also important that children grasp the fact that water is a finite resource and that its treatment and getting it to homes and work places cost money. This knowledge prepares the way to understanding that, although global access to clean water is largely determined by geographical location, climate and weather, there are also political, economic and social dimensions to its availability and use.

Reasoning and information processing skills

❑ Brainstorm what the children know about where water comes from.

❑ Give them access to books and websites where they can find information to check their ideas. Most water authorities now have websites with pages for children.

❑ Give them copies of the river illustration on photocopiable Sheet 18. Ask them to write a paragraph using the correct geographical terminology to describe the journey of this river from source to mouth.

❑ Use these questions to develop understanding:
  - How is the water along the course of this river used?
  - Is there any evidence for how the river was used in the past?
  - What do you think are 'good' uses of the river?
  - What are not good uses of the river?
  - Why does the river change shape along its course?
  - Can you see any evidence of how people have changed the shape and flow of the river?

❑ Discuss how water gets to our homes. How is it made fit to drink? Does all the water we use need to be treated? Encourage the understanding that water is not a 'free' resource despite the fact that it rains a lot in the UK.

❑ Ask the children to carry out an audit of water use in their home for one week. Discuss with the class the uses they are going to measure. How many baths do family members take? How many times to they flush the toilet? Typical usage quantities used can be found on websites (see References on page 72). They can use the table on photocopiable Sheet 19, adding other uses as they wish.

Evaluation skills

❏ After one week ask the children to comment on their usage of water. Are they surprised by the amount they have used? They can compare their water usage with national statistics at www.water.org.uk/information/statistics. In what ways could they reduce their water use without going unclean or thirsty?

I suppose I should turn off the tap while I am brushing my teeth.

❏ Give the children access to the following website which tells people how to conserve water. www.waterwise.fortune-cookie.com/homes. Suggestions include:

– Use a water butt in the garden to collect rainwater.
– Have a shower instead of a bath. This can save up to 400 litres of water a week.
– Fix leaking taps. A dripping tap can waste up to 90 litres of water per week.
– Use the dishwasher only when you have a full load.
– Fill the kettle with only as much water as you need. Use left over water on house plants.

❏ Ask the children to evaluate these suggestions. Which do they think can be done easily? Which would be more difficult? Which cost money? Which are more about changing habits?

❏ Tell the children that the average household could save the equivalent of 15 baths of water every week – 1,350 litres – by putting into practice some of these ideas.

Links with the Geography Scheme of Work

This activity supports the learning objectives in Unit 11, 'Water', and aspects of the learning objectives in Unit 14, 'Investigating rivers'.

ESD focus

This activity helps children appreciate that they have choices in the way they use fresh water – a precious and finite resource – and that these choices can affect other people and the environment in different ways.

Investigating rivers

River pollution

Introduction

Any study of water and rivers will include investigating the causes and effects of pollution. It is obviously vital that young children understand why it is important that water pollution is prevented and how this can be done. Developing their thinking skills is key to this understanding.

Enquiry skills

❑ Brainstorm what children think pollution is and what causes it. This could be done as a circle time activity with the ground rule that all opinions are listened to respectfully. Record the ideas that they are happy with. Discuss the different sources of pollution – from chemicals, sewage, litter, noise and so on.

❑ Now give them copies of the river illustration on photocopiable Sheet 20. Ask them to identify all the sources of pollution that they can see here. It might be helpful to suggest they look for examples under headings such as farming, industry and leisure activities.

Reasoning skills

❑ Organise the children into groups and ask them to discuss which they think are the most serious and the least serious sources of pollution. For example, allowing dangerous chemicals to get into the water can seriously affect people and wildlife all down the river. It is fairly easy to remove dumped items and to stop people using noisy boats.

❑ Tell them to select nine sources and then rank them according to seriousness with the most serious at the top and the least serious at the bottom.

Creative thinking and evaluation skills

❏ Ask the children to discuss and agree a creative plan to prevent further pollution from the most serious sources in their ranking. They could base it on the model below.

Model
1. Identify source of pollution (farm, factory, general public).
2. Find out who is responsible (landowner, board of directors, local authority).
3. Research whether there are any laws about this type of pollution (environmental agency website, local planning department).
4. Decide on most appropriate methods of telling people responsible (letter, leaflets, posters).
5. Record and evaluate results. Plan next stage.

❏ Swap the plans between the groups and then ask each group to evaluate the plan in front of them, using questions such as:

 – Do they think this plan will work?
 – Who will put it into practice?
 – Will it cost a lot of money?
 – Who or what might suffer if this plan is implemented?
 – Who or what might benefit if this plan is implemented?

Links with the Geography Scheme of Work

This activity develops the fourth learning objective in Unit 14, 'Investigating rivers: What is this river like? How is it changing and why?'

ESD focus

This activity develops understanding that human actions can harm or enhance the ability of wildlife to survive and flourish, and that they can also have a profound impact on people now and in the future.

Investigating coasts

Coastal erosion

Objectives

- To use enquiry and reasoning skills to identify why the coast changes.

- To make suggestions how the effects of erosion can be limited, critically evaluating them.

Resources

- Photocopiable Sheets 21 and 22 (pages 66 and 67)

Introduction

An intensive block of coastal fieldwork can deepen children's geographical insight and understanding considerably. It also enables the integration of appropriate cross-curricular issues with many more opportunities to develop and strengthen thinking skills. If a fieldwork trip is not possible, the same thinking skills can be developed using the illustration provided.

Enquiry skills

❑ Give the children copies of photocopiable Sheet 21 (page 66). Brainstorm questions the children might want to ask about the illustration. These might include:
  - Why do the cliffs look like this?
  - How does the sea affect the cliff?
  - Who lives here? (Think of people and wildlife.)
  - Who comes to visit this place?

❑ Talk about what causes the cliffs to erode, how and why this happens. Provide books and other resources to help the children develop this understanding. Explain that although some parts of the British coastline are eroding, particularly along the east coast, other parts of the coastline are extending into the sea, for example parts of the Welsh coastline.

Is it safe to live so close to the edge?

Reasoning skills

❏ Extend the children's thinking by posing questions such as:
  - Why do you think people come to this bit of coast?
  - What provision has been made for wildlife?
  - Do you think this bit of coastline might be, or become, dangerous? Why?
  - Could ships come near to this coastline?
  - Is there any evidence of what is being done to prevent the coast eroding?

❏ Next, read through the 'Coastline in danger' scenario on photocopiable Sheet 22 (page 67). Find the Yorkshire coast on a map of Great Britain. This story is based around the Holderness area. Talk about what sort of materials and work would be needed to protect these cliffs.

❏ Divide the class into groups and ask each group to discuss what the local people should do.
  - Should money be spent on reinforcing the cliff? Why?
  - Will the reinforcement be sufficient to stop further erosion?
  - What other action could be taken to protect the cliff from erosion?
  - What other, less expensive, action could be taken to protect people, their homes and their livelihoods?

❏ Let each group present the reasons for their conclusions to the whole class. Discuss the reasons given. Was there a consensus on what should be done? It might be that they decide a lot more research is needed before the best option can be agreed.

Links with the Geography Scheme of Work

This activity supports Unit 23, 'Investigating coasts', in particular the learning objectives: 'How do waves shape coastal environments?' and 'How does human activity affect coastal environments?'

ESD focus

This activity helps children distinguish between the environmental effects of natural and human activity, and how the latter can exacerbate or diminish the impact of the former. It also develops understanding that situations change and therefore care and caution are required before taking action.

Contrasting localities

Objectives

- To use information processing skills to locate the source of food we buy.
- To ask questions about the countries of origin.
- To investigate why food travels so far, and think about other solutions.

Resources

- Clipboards
- Access to the Internet

Where does our food come from?

Introduction

One way to make children aware of contrasting localities is to investigate where our food comes from, exploring how global trade works, and the impact this has on people and the environment. It also develops understanding of our rights and responsibilities as global citizens.

Information processing skills

❑ Arrange a supermarket visit to look at the fruit and vegetables. Make notes of where each fruit or vegetable comes from.

❑ Back in the classroom, locate the countries on a map. For example, the children below have discovered that some green beans come from Kenya. Find the place on the map and ask these questions:

- – Where is this place?
- – What do you think the weather is like?
- – How many kilometres is this place from the UK?

Reasoning skills

❏ Ask the children to work in small groups to choose five fruits or vegetables to investigate more deeply. Give them these questions to focus their investigation:

- How long do you think it took for this product to get from the country where it was grown to your supermarket?
- What sort of transport was probably used?
- What might be the effects on the environment of the transport used?
- How do you think the product was kept fresh during its journey?

❏ When they have written down all their ideas, discuss them with the whole class and then ask each group how many of their fruits and vegetables could be grown in this country. Discuss their answers, checking the facts if there are any doubts.

❏ Do the children think that we should eat only fruit and vegetables grown in this country? Use copies of the consequences wheel (as shown on page 26) to think through the consequences of doing this for one fruit or vegetable. They should think about the economic, political, social and environmental effects, locally and globally.

Evaluation and creative thinking skills

❏ What conclusions do the children draw from this exercise? If they were in the Department of Trade and Industry, how would they advise the government as to the most sustainable way of supplying people in the UK with fresh fruit and vegetables? Ideas might include giving more support to farmers' markets where locally grown food is brought into nearby towns, or encouraging more farmers to set up farm shops.

❏ Discuss the ideas offered. Encourage the children to ask each other questions to critically evaluate the ideas suggested. If possible, agree one or two good ideas and write a letter to the local MP giving the details.

Links with the Geography Scheme of Work

This activity links those learning objectives to do with extending children's understanding of different places and how we are connected to them. For example, 'How do we find out about other places?' in Unit 24, 'Passport to the world', and learning objectives 1, 2, 6 and 7 in Unit 10, 'A village in India'.

ESD focus

This activity helps children explore global economic interdependence and how consumer choice has profound social, economic and environmental impacts around the globe.

Tourism

Introduction

Building on work done at Key Stage 1 on holidays, this activity deepens children's knowledge and understanding of localities in different parts of the world. A theme on tourism can help them appreciate our global interdependence, who wins and who loses and how the environment is affected.

Reasoning skills

❏ Organise the children into pairs and give them copies of the newspaper report on the photocopiable sheet on page 68 to read. (Source: adapted from an article in 'The Sunday Times', 27 January 2002.)

Enquiry and reasoning skills

❏ Brainstorm questions children will need to consider to investigate this report, such as:

- Where is Koh Phi Phi?
- What would you expect it to be like?
- What does this article tell you about what it is really like?
- Why is this place like this?
- What do you think it would be like to visit Koh Phi Phi?
- How do you think people who live there feel about the tourists?
- What are the similarities and differences between Koh Phi Phi and a resort you know in the UK?

❏ Discuss the children's answers. Ask them to think about what can be done by a) the people of Thailand, and b) the tourists who visit the islands.

❏ Discuss where they could find information to help them. Consider approaching tourist companies and environmental organisations to get a rounded picture.

Creative thinking and evaluation skills

- Ask the children to work in small groups to design and make a leaflet on 'Travel Tips' for responsible tourism. This might include headings such as:

  - When to go;
  - Choice of transport;
  - Water and energy use;
  - Take care of the environment;
  - Respect local customs;
  - Don't buy wildlife souvenirs.

  (Useful websites are given on page 72 to help the children in their research.)

- Encourage the children to critically evaluate each other's ideas, thinking about the economic, political, social and environmental dimensions. They could agree on a final design for making into a poster for the school entrance hall, or to put in the school magazine. It could be illustrated to make it more eye-catching.

Links with the Geography Scheme of Work

This activity provides a resource for developing the learning objective in Unit 15, 'The mountain environment', which asks children to think about the good and bad effects of tourism.

ESD focus

This activity helps children to appreciate the short- and long-term effects of human activity on natural systems and how these have to be balanced by the needs of human social and economic development.

Different places

Objectives

- To use a range of enquiry skills to plan a trip to a mountain area.

- To evaluate the methods of travel and their effects on the environment.

Resources

- Photocopiable Sheet 24 (page 69)

- Atlases, encyclopedias

- Access to the internet

Planning a journey

Introduction

Units of work about contrasting localities and environments could include planning a trip to a mountain environment. The focus for this activity is the Himalayas, but there are opportunities to extend the work to contrasting mountain environments.

Information processing skills

❏ To prepare the children for this activity, ask them to research a proposed trip to Katmandu in the Himalayas, using questions such as:
- – Where is Katmandu?
- – What is it like there?
- – What do people do there?
- – What is the weather/climate like?

❏ Give them copies of photocopiable Sheet 24 (page 69) which provides more ideas for things to research, and discuss what they will need to do their research. Make atlases, relevant books and encyclopedias available. Useful websites are listed in the reference section on page 72.

❏ When they have completed their research they can fill in the planning sheet.

Enquiry skills

❏ Talk about where there are other mountain environments in the world. Choose two from different parts of the world and discuss how they are the same as, and different from, the Himalayas. For example, how high are they? Do they all have the same amount of ice and snow? How do local people use the lower slopes?

❏ A particular focus might be how the weather varies and what impact this has on both the people who live there and visitors. Ask the children to collect data about weather in their chosen mountain areas and to think about how weather might vary from season to season.

❏ Record these differences. The planning sheet for Katmandu could be used for planning two other mountain holidays – say to the Peak District in Britain or the Pyrenees between France and Spain – so the similarities and differences could be drawn out more clearly.

Reasoning and evaluation skills

❑ In groups, the children can investigate how they will get to their chosen mountain destination: overland, by sea or by air. Which would be the most convenient in terms of journey time and cost? The most interesting? The least damaging to the environment in terms of fuel use, air and noise pollution?

❑ Give them appropriate scale maps to plot their journey thinking about the location of airports, ferry crossings, train and bus stations. Encourage them to share and discuss their reasons for their choice of route and methods of transport.

❑ Hold a plenary session for each group to feed back their agreed reasons for a specific travel plan.

Links with the Geography Scheme of Work

This activity relates to aspects of the learning objectives in Unit 15, 'The mountain environment', particularly the investigative work, and the final objective, 'What would I need to plan a camping holiday in this area?' It also links to the last two objectives in Unit 18, 'Connecting ourselves to the world'.

ESD focus

This activity helps to develop understanding of diversity in terms of human society and biodiversity. It also provides scope to discuss the environmental impact of travel.

Different places

Finding out about rainforests

Objective

- To develop understanding about rainforest environments using a range of thinking skills.

Resources

- Photocopiable Sheet 25 (page 70)

- Books and other resources about rainforests

- Access to the Internet

Introduction

Most children come to school with a lot of knowledge about rainforests gleaned from stories and television programmes. The following activity serves as a geographical approach to the topic, giving them an opportunity to share their knowledge and think through what more they need to know.

Creative thinking skills

❑ Ask the children to spend a few minutes thinking about their perception of a rainforest. Don't make any resources available at this stage. Then give them copies of the photocopiable sheet on page 70 to record their thoughts and ideas in text and drawings.

❑ When they are happy with what they have done, tell them to put the sheets away in a folder.

Enquiry skills

❑ As a class, brainstorm questions that the children want to ask about rainforests – these will form the basis of their exploration. They might include:

- – What is a rainforest like?
- – How is it different from a forest in Europe?
- – Where in the world are rainforests?
- – Are they all the same?
- – What lives there?

❑ Agree on ten questions and their order of importance. The children might add supplementary questions as they think through the structure of what they want to find out.

❑ Write all the questions on labels and tack them to a large display board. Provide a range of resources – books, CD-Roms and websites – to help them find answers to their questions. As they find answers, this information can be placed underneath the questions.

Reasoning and evaluation skills

❑ At the end of this research, ask the children to look at their completed photocopiable sheets. How has their perception of a rainforest changed? Divide the class into groups and ask them to compare and discuss how their views have changed. Ask them to write down the main reasons why their views have changed. Encourage them to explain why, as clearly as possible.

❑ Now that they have so much more information, ask the children:

– Why do they think the rainforest is important?
– Why is it being destroyed?
– What can be done to prevent further loss in the future?

The photocopiable sheet is based on an idea in an article in *Primary Geographer*, July 1999.

Links with the Geography Scheme of Work

This activity can be the focus for the learning objectives in Unit 15, replacing mountain with rainforest.

ESD focus

This activity helps children to develop understanding and appreciation of the richness of rainforest biodiversity and why we should protect it. It also underlines the interdependence of people and the natural environment.

Name _____

Name _____

Put a tick when you see one of these.

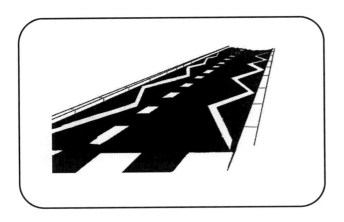

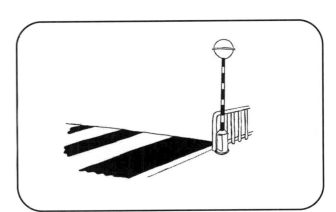

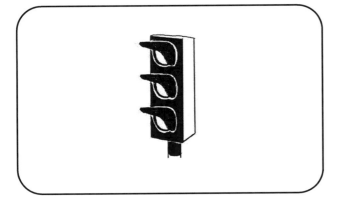

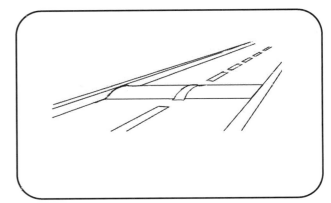

Name _____

Traffic survey sheet

Type of transport		Tally
car		
lorry		
bus		
bike		
van		
motorbike		
taxi		
fire engine		

Thinking skills: Geography and ESD

Name _____

The seaside

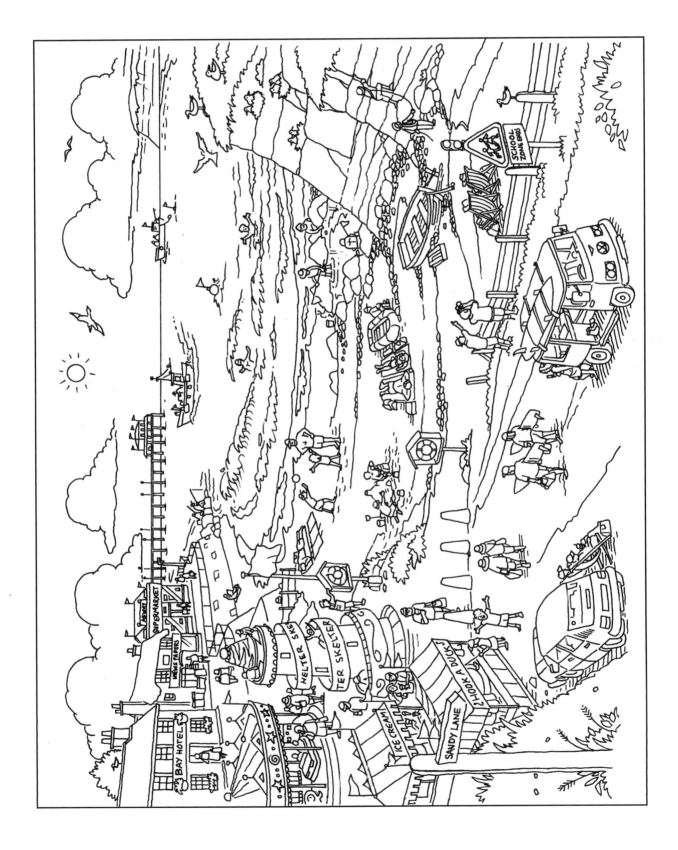

Name _____

My favourite holiday place

I would like to go to	
I would get there by	
This is what I would see there	
This is what I could do there	
I like this place because	

Thinking skills: Geography and ESD

Name _____

I am Anusibuno

I am seven years old. I live in a village called Zuo, in northern Ghana. I live with my mother and father and four sisters in rooms which are built within a circular wall.

Our house is made from mud and wood. We live together with other people in a compound. We have five rooms: my father's room, a kitchen area, the grinding-stone room, and two others which we use for storage, sleeping and living rooms.

I wake up around 5.30am.

Every morning I sweep our part of the compound, fetch water from the pump with my sisters, then I help my mother to make breakfast.

We often have a sort of porridge called pumpuka for breakfast. It is made from ground millet. I help put the pumpuka into bowls and then my sisters, mother and I sit down outside to eat it.

Name _____

I am Anusibuno

Then I go to wash in the water we have collected from the pump. I dry myself and rub shea butter on my skin to protect it from the sun and wind.

I put on my dress and walk to school.

I started school two years ago and now I'm in Class P2. There are ten children in my class. We also have to share the classroom with the younger children.

I like my teacher, Mary-Jo. I like doing maths best of all. I enjoy the singing and dancing too.

I play with my sisters and friends who live in the compound. We like playing hopscotch. We also make toys from clay and put them in the sun to dry.

Adapted from a case study from www.oxfam.org.uk/coolplanet/ontheline

Name _____

Finding out about another place

How our lives are different from Anusibuno's life	
Anusibuno's life	Our lives
Home	
Getting up	
Breakfast	
Washing	
School	
Play	

Name _____

How is our locality changing?

RECORDING SHEET			
Key features today	18th century	19th century	20th century
Church			
Park			
Town hall			
Shopping centre			
School			

Thinking skills: Geography and ESD

Name _____

More shops

There are plans to develop a new shopping centre in an open area behind the town hall where a market has been held once a week for many years.

The town already has a large shopping precinct, but there is great competition from a nearby town that has a much better shopping area. The council is concerned that more people will choose to shop there, and that local shops and businesses will suffer.

There is to be a public meeting so that the views of all the different interest groups can be discussed before a final decision is made.

Name _____

Land use

Development company
We believe that we can bring much more business to this community. Everyone will benefit from the new shops. People will have more choice and people from other areas will come to spend their money here.

Local shopkeepers
We are very concerned. We will lose customers and local people will lose the small local shops that they like. There will be less choice because big shops all sell the same ranges of goods.

Local arts group
We think that the community needs a place where they can come to listen to music, see art displays from different cultures, see plays and dance performances. Young and old could come here to learn new skills and enjoy themselves.

Environmental group
Another shopping mall would cause more traffic and pollution. We need to preserve some green spaces where people can relax and enjoy nature. It would be better to have a farmers' market, where people could buy food grown locally.

Residents' association
Most of us have lived here for a long time. We fear that more shops will make our community look just like any other community. We want to keep some of the old places that give our community its character.

Thinking skills: Geography and ESD

Name _____

Waste and recycling

Draw a line from each product to its correct recycling bin.

What is paper made from?		What is glass made from?	
Grass	☐	Sand	☐
Trees	☐	Shells	☐
Minerals	☐	Bones	☐

What is plastic made from?		What is aluminium made from?	
Plant material	☐	Iron	☐
Petroleum	☐	A mineral called bauxite	☐
Rubber	☐	Copper	☐

Name _____

Early settlers

VILLAGE FEATURES				
Geographical feature				
Sheltered valley				
Good farmland				
River crossing				
Fresh water				
Away from flood plain				
Near coast				
Near fort or castle				

Thinking skills: Geography and ESD

Name _____

Ténéga – my village

By Bamana Kadira Christophe

My village is called Ténéga. When a man called Ti'a Nadada first came here a long time ago, he saw the valley and the river and he made his home beside it. He called the river by his own name.

Ténéga is made up of five separate neighbourhoods – Balley, Bidigou, Natoun, Djofaga and Djérégou.

Balley is next to the river Nadada. As you walk alongside the Nadada you hear all sorts of sounds – a mill working, people arguing, other people chatting to one another. There is a primary school in the neighbourhood. There are round huts, a lot of clay houses, and some brick-built houses where the chiefs and the government officials live. The name Balley means riverbank.

Bidigou is the part of Ténéga where the ceremonies take place. There are still some of the traditional-style round huts with small doorways. You can still see the ceremonial huts with the straw roof and no doors. There is a Catholic church in this part of the village, near the village cemetery. There is a primary school in Bidigou too.

Name _____

Ténéga – my village

Djofaga is where the village headman lives. It is the built-up centre of the village. There is a secondary school and the clinic here. A small market takes place every Saturday and Sunday. Rich people live here in brick-built houses, with two storeys. Djofaga means to sleep upstairs.

Natoun is where the buffaloes used to live. This was where Ti'a had a farm. He used to send his second son out to chase the wild animals away. Natoun means the place where the buffaloes are. There is a weather station here which is often visited by outsiders. There is a primary school here as well.

Djérégou has a sacred wood called Tikpoume Ragou, or the wood of the rains. When there hasn't been any rain in Ténéga the old people chant sacred songs in the wood to ask what's wrong. It begins to rain, even before they have got back home.

People in Ténéga grow maize, millet, sorghum and groundnuts. During the rainy season crops like millet cover the whole of the village. The village is completely green. The village can only be seen in the dry season after the millet stalks have been cut down. Every family has seven or eight fields including at least one orchard of oil palms, which is the village's main tree. The Europeans insisted that our forefathers should plant mango trees, which is why we have mango trees in my village.

Name _____

Ténéga – my village

Some people weave baskets and sieves which the white people find attractive. The oil palm is the most important tree in the village because it can be used to make a lot of different things. The long stem provides timber for building while the branches can be used for sieves and baskets. There are clusters of fruit which are used to make palm-oil and palm-kernel oil.

The people of Ténéga are traders as well. Men and women sell sieves, baskets and agricultural produce in the markets. The women barter red oil and sieves in exchange for rice, millet and so on. They buy chickens, goats and sheep for the ceremonies.

Adapted from a case study from www.oxfam.org.uk/coolplanet/ontheline

Name _____

Village features

Neighbourhood	Features
Balley	
Bidigou	
Natoun	
Djofaga	
Djérégou	

Name _____

A river

Name _____

How much water do we use?

WATER AUDIT			
Water use	Litres used	Times used	Total number of litres per week
bath			
shower			
cleaning teeth			
toilet flush			
washing hands			
drinking			

Name _____

River pollution

Name _____

Coastal erosion

Thinking skills: Geography and ESD

Coastline in danger

A section of beautiful coastline in Yorkshire is in danger of being seriously eroded as the last few years of winter gales and storms have pounded the chalk cliff relentlessly. The cliff is now eroding at approximately two metres a year.

Peter and Marion Smith have a small guest house, 100 metres from the cliff edge. For over ten years they have run a very successful business as this is an area of great natural beauty, and butterfly and bird enthusiasts come here year after year. They want to expand their business by building a large hotel. This will bring more tourists to the area and increase the use of the coastal footpath.

Many other families live in the village nearby. They also depend on the tourist trade, although more people now commute to the nearest town because a big information and communications company came there recently and they need staff.

Over the last five years a great deal of money has been used to build sea defences. But these have been useless in the face of huge powerful waves. Scientists warn that because of global warming, extreme weather conditions are more likely to occur.

It is now proposed that the only solution is to reinforce the cliff. This is likely to cost many thousands of pounds.

Name _____

Thai beaches die in tourist invasion

Hollywood movie is the cause of the potential loss of a way of life to whole island community.

The Thai island Koh Phi Phi was made famous by the film 'The Beach'. But since Leonardo Di Caprio and the cast left, it has become overrun by tourists. Local officials are now calling for the island to be closed to visitors to save its fragile ecosystem.

According to the local tourist police, Koh Phi Phi has been spoiled by pollution and hordes of visitors. They suggest that it be sealed up for two years while the mess is cleared up.

The tourism authority of Thailand is not happy about this. Tourists bring in about £160,000 a day. They ask, 'What about the residents who make their living from tourism? What about the tour operators who invest in the island? And what about

Inhabitants of the once idyllic island which is threatened with closure to tourists.

the country, which is in need of foreign exchange?'

Environmental campaigners say that a nearby island has already been destroyed. The biggest blow came when tourists were given rides on elephants on the beach and across the shallow coral reefs. The weight of the elephants rapidly destroyed coral that had taken 8,000 years to grow.

Glossary

Ecosystem – a group of plants and animals living together in one place. Removing one plant or animal can upset the balance and threaten the survival of them all.

Name _____

Planning a trip to Katmandu

Questions	Findings
How far is Katmandu from your home? *Work this out using an atlas.*	
Is Katmandu in the same time zone as Britain? *Use an atlas to find out. Calculate what the time difference is and think about the implications of this for the proposed trip.*	
What time of year will you go? *Think about factors such as the weather and events that you might like to enjoy such as local festivals.*	
What will you need to take? *Think about the climate and what you plan to do. What sort of clothing and footwear will you need?*	
Are there things you need to find out before you go? *For example, passport/visa requirements, vaccinations, information on local customs (ie what is, and is not, acceptable), whether the water is drinkable and so on.*	

Thinking skills: Geography and ESD

Name _____

Finding out about rainforests

My perception of a rainforest

What I know ...	What I guess ...
What I want to find out ...	**My picture of ...**

References – 1

Useful addresses

WWF-UK
Panda House, Weyside Park, Godalming, GU7 1XR
www.wwf.org.uk

The Geographical Association
160 Solly Street, Sheffield, S1 4BF
www.geography.org.uk

Oxfam
274 Banbury Road, Oxford, OX2 7DZ
www.oxfam.org.uk

Development Education Association
33 Corsham Street, London N1 6DR
www.dea.org.uk

Books and teaching resources

Resources for Key Stages 1 and 2 (Geography Guidance series) Rachel Bowles, The Geographical Association, 1999. This is a very comprehensive list of printed resources and computer software.

Primary Internet Investigator – Introducing sustainability issues through the internet, WWF-UK, 2001. Contains activities and related websites for teaching about water and rivers, waste management and traffic issues.

Thinking Skills – A teacher's guide, Mike Jeffries and Trevor Hancock, Hopscotch Educational Publishing, 2002. A comprehensive guide with practical classroom activities.

Thinking through Geography, Simon Chandler and David Leat, Chris Kington Publishing, 2001

Citizenship for the Future – A Practical Classroom Guide, David Hicks, WWF-UK, 2001

Making it Happen – Agenda 21 and schools, Gillian Symons, WWF-UK, 1998

Focus on… Photopack series WWF-UK. *Rivers*, Jane Featherstone, 1999 and *Coasts*, Prue Poulton, 1998 Each pack contains: 12 A4 colour photocards, an A2 poster with a board game on the reverse and a teachers' guide with photocopiable resource sheets.

'Exploring…' software series. WWF -UK. *Rivers*, Christiane Dorion and Patricia Kendell, 1999;

Coasts, Prue Poulton, 1997; *Towns and cities*, Trish Sandbach and Richard Borowski, 2001. Each pack contains a teachers' guide with photocopiable resource sheets; an A2 poster with a board game on the reverse; and hotline support and a site licence. Hardware requirements: Windows Version 3.1 or higher, VGA monitor (SVGA recommended).

Books for children

Exploring Towns and *Exploring Villages* (Landmark series), Wayland, 1997

Rivers, *Coasts* and *Settlements* (Earth Alert! series), Hodder Wayland

Websites

The following websites were all active at the time of going to press, but addresses can change and pages can be removed, edited or replaced. An indication of target audience is given: **T** = teachers; **C** = children. Most might need some teacher guidance.

www.wwflearning.co.uk   T

WWF-UK's dedicated site for teachers includes news, activities and a resource bank covering a range of sustainable development issues.

www.learn.co.uk   T

The 'Guardian' site for teachers with much material to support the National Curriculum and schemes of work.

www.nc.uk.net   T

This QCA site provides guidance for teachers on education for sustainable development.

www.panda.org   T

Search here for information on climate change, tourism, rainforest management, endangered species and much more.

References - 2

Websites to support activities in this book

Information on sustainable development issues

www.oxfam.org.uk/coolplanet/ontheline
T, C

Background information about Ghana and Togo.

www.childrenoftheearth.org   C

An interactive site with information about animals, logging and rainforests

www.rainforestalliance.org   C

Much useful information about rainforests – why and how they are being destroyed, their importance and what can be done to manage what remains sustainably.

www.environment-agency.gov.uk   T, C

This site has much useful information to support activities in this book. It also has pages for children including animation and film sequences.

Taking action

www.wwf.org.uk/core   T, C

(Once in the website click on 'Take action' and then on 'Rethink'.) Acting responsibly as a tourist at home and abroad and as a shopper.

www.globalactionplan.org.uk   T, C

How to plan action in school to save water, manage waste, and use transport more sustainably.

Waste management

www.greenchoices.org.uk   T, C

Many practical ideas for environmentally friendly consumer choices.

www.wastewatch.org.uk   T, C

This has a section for children and information about paper, glass, wood, aluminium cans and many other materials and products.

Traffic issues

www.dft.gov.uk   T

Statistics on transport.

www.roads.dft.gov.uk   T

Information on child road safety campaigns.

www.sustrans.co.uk   T, C

Projects to encourage children to walk and cycle to school.

www.youngtransnet.org.uk   C

Ideas for how children can improve transport in their local area.

Water issues

www.e4s.org.uk   C

This site has an interactive water cycle diagram, and activities on waste management.

www.water.org.uk   T

Has links to water authorities and other agencies.

Weather

www.meto.gov.uk   T, C

The Met Office site containing many ideas and links to learning resources.

www.weather.co.uk   T, C

National forecasts are available here.

www.cirrus.sprl.umich.edu/wxnet/   T, C

Weather maps for across the world with links to many other weather-related sites.

www.bbc.co.uk/weather   T, C

A comprehensive site for the UK and the world.